SINGLE-PARENT FAMILIES

Families Today

Adoptive Families

Disability and Families

Foster Families

Homelessness and Families

Immigrant Families

Incarceration and Families

LGBT Families

Military Families

Multigenerational Families

Multiracial Families

Single-Parent Families

Teen Parents

Families Today

SINGLE-PARENT FAMILIES

H.W. Poole

MASON CREST

Mason Crest
450 Parkway Drive, Suite D
Broomall, PA 19008
www.masoncrest.com

MTM Publishing, Inc.
435 West 23rd Street, #8C
New York, NY 10011
www.mtmpublishing.com

President: Valerie Tomaselli
Vice President, Book Development: Hilary Poole
Designer: Annemarie Redmond
Copyeditor: Peter Jaskowiak
Editorial Assistant: Andrea St. Aubin

Series ISBN: 978-1-4222-3612-3
Hardback ISBN: 978-1-4222-3623-9
E-Book ISBN: 978-1-4222-8267-0

Library of Congress Cataloging-in-Publication Data
Names: Poole, Hilary W., author.
Title: Single-parent families / by H.W. Poole.
Description: Broomall, PA : Mason Crest [2017] | Series: Families Today | Includes index.
Identifiers: LCCN 2016004547| ISBN 9781422236239 (hardback) | ISBN 9781422236123
(series) | ISBN 9781422282670 (e-book)
Subjects: LCSH: Single-parent families—Juvenile literature. | Children of single
parents—Juvenile literature. | Families—Juvenile literature.
Classification: LCC HQ759.915 .P66 2017 | DDC 306.85/6—dc23
LC record available at http://lccn.loc.gov/2016004547

Printed and bound in the United States of America.

First printing
9 8 7 6 5 4 3 2 1

TABLE OF CONTENTS

Series Introduction 7

Chapter One: Who Are Single Parents? 11

Chapter Two: Divorce and Single Parents 19

Chapter Three: Single Parents and Economics 29

Chapter Four: Are Single Parents Good Parents? 37

Further Reading 44

Series Glossary 45

Index 47

About the Author 48

Photo Credits 48

Key Icons to Look for:

Words to Understand: These words with their easy-to-understand definitions will increase the reader's understanding of the text, while building vocabulary skills.

Sidebars: This boxed material within the main text allows readers to build knowledge, gain insights, explore possibilities, and broaden their perspectives by weaving together additional information to provide realistic and holistic perspectives.

Research Projects: Readers are pointed toward areas of further inquiry connected to each chapter. Suggestions are provided for projects that encourage deeper research and analysis.

Text-Dependent Questions: These questions send the reader back to the text for more careful attention to the evidence presented there.

Series Glossary of Key Terms: This back-of-the-book glossary contains terminology used throughout the series. Words found here increase the reader's ability to read and comprehend higher-level books and articles in this field.

In the 21st century, families are more diverse than ever before.

SERIES INTRODUCTION

Our vision of "the traditional family" is not nearly as time-honored as one might think. The standard of a mom, a dad, and a couple of kids in a nice house with a white-picket fence is a relic of the 1950s—the heart of the baby boom era. The tumult of the Great Depression followed by a global war caused many Americans to long for safety and predictability—whether such stability was real or not. A newborn mass media was more than happy to serve up this image, in the form of TV shows like *Leave It To Beaver* and *The Adventures of Ozzie and Harriet*. Interestingly, even back in the "glory days" of the traditional family, things were never as simple as they seemed. For example, a number of the classic "traditional" family shows—such as *The Andy Griffith Show, My Three Sons,* and a bit later, *The Courtship of Eddie's Father*—were actually focused on single-parent families.

Sure enough, by the 1960s our image of the "perfect family" was already beginning to fray at the seams. The women's movement, the gay rights movement, and—perhaps more than any single factor—the advent of "no fault" divorce meant that the illusion of the Cleaver family would become harder and harder to maintain. By the early 21st century, only about 7 percent of all family households were traditional—defined as a married couple with children where *only* the father works outside the home.

As the number of these traditional families has declined, "nontraditional" arrangements have increased. There are more single parents, more gay and lesbian parents, and more grandparents raising grandchildren than ever before. Multiracial families—created either through interracial relationships or adoption—are also increasing. Meanwhile, the transition to an all-volunteer military force has meant that there are more kids growing up in military families than there were in the past. Each of these topics is treated in a separate volume in this set.

While some commentators bemoan the decline of the traditional family, others argue that, overall, the recognition of new family arrangements has brought more good than bad. After all, if very few people live like the Cleavers anyway, isn't it better to be honest about that fact? Surely, holding up the traditional family as an ideal to which all should aspire only serves to stigmatize kids whose lives differ from that standard. After all, no children can be held responsible for whatever family they find themselves in; all they can do is grow up as best they can. These books take the position that every family—no matter what it looks like—has the potential to be a successful family.

That being said, challenges and difficulties arise in every family, and nontraditional ones are no exception. For example, single parents tend to be less well off financially than married parents are, and this has long-term impacts on their children. Meanwhile, teenagers who become parents tend to let their educations suffer, which damages their income potential and career possibilities, as well as risking the future educational attainment of their babies. There are some 400,000 children in the foster care system at any given time. We know that the uncertainty of foster care creates real challenges when it comes to both education and emotional health.

Furthermore, some types of "nontraditional" families are ones we wish did not have to exist at all. For example, an estimated 1.6 million children experience homelessness at some point in their lives. At least 40 percent of homeless kids are lesbian, gay, bisexual, or transgender teens who were turned out of their homes because of their orientation. Meanwhile, the United States incarcerates more people than any other nation in the world—about 2.7 million kids (1 in 28) have an incarcerated parent. It would be absurd to pretend that such situations are not extremely stressful and, often, detrimental to kids who have to survive them.

The goal of this set, then, is twofold. First, we've tried to describe the history and shape of various nontraditional families in such a way that kids who aren't familiar with them will be able to not only understand, but empathize. We also present demographic information that may be useful for students who are dipping their toes into introductory sociology concepts.

Second, we have tried to speak specifically to the young people who are living in these nontraditional families. The series strives to address these kids as

Meeting challenges and overcoming them together can make families stronger.

sympathetically and supportively as possible. The volumes look at some of the typical problems that kids in these situations face, and where appropriate, they offer advice and tips for how these kids might get along better in whatever situation confronts them.

Obviously, no single book—whether on disability, the military, divorce, or some other topic—can hope to answer every question or address every problem. To that end, a "Further Reading" section at the back of each book attempts to offer some places to look next. We have also listed appropriate crisis hotlines, for anyone with a need more immediate than can be addressed by a library.

Whether your students have a project to complete or a problem to solve, we hope they will be able to find clear, empathic information about nontraditional families in these pages.

—H. W. Poole

When people hear the term "single parent," they tend to think of single moms. But in fact there are almost 2 million single dads in the United States.

Chapter One

WHO ARE SINGLE PARENTS?

When a family is made up of a mother, a father, and one child or more, that's called a "nuclear family." The term comes from physics: an atom has a nucleus at the center with electrons and protons circling it. The idea is that the nuclear family is the center of our lives.

Comparing a family to atoms kind of makes it sound natural and eternal—as if families have always been this way and always should be this way. But if you study the history of the family, you'll find that nuclear families have not been around all that long. Families used to be much bigger, for one thing. A "family" usually included at least three generations (grandparents, parents, and kids), as well as aunts, uncles, and cousins. Nowadays, we call this an "extended family" as a way of contrasting it with the smaller, nuclear family. But historically, large families all lived near each other and depended on one another.

Words to Understand

annulment: when a marriage is declared to have been invalid; legally, it is as though the marriage never happened.

secular: nonreligious.

Today, only 46 percent of kids live in what would be described as a nuclear family. In fact, increasing numbers of kids are being raised by one parent, rather than two—not adhering to the classic definition of a nuclear family.

TYPES OF SINGLE PARENTS

The basic situation of all single parents is the same: one adult, without a partner, is raising one or more children. But within that general description, there are many different single parents, and many ways to become one.

Never Married. Of all single parents, about 49 percent were never married at all. There are a variety of reasons for this. Sometimes two people are in a relationship and the woman gets pregnant, but the couple decides not to marry. Many teen parents fall into the "never married" category. In 2013 there were more than 270,000 babies born to mothers aged 15 to 19—and of those, about 80 percent of the mothers were unmarried. (For much more on teen parents, please see the book *Teen Parents* in this series.)

The vast majority of pregnant teenagers will become single mothers.

CHILDREN IN SINGLE-PARENT FAMILIES, BY ETHNICITY

		2010	2011	2012	2013
American Indian	Number	350,000	355,000	345,000	329,000
	Percent	52	53	53	52
Asian or Pacific Islander	Number	539,000	559,000	579,000	557,000
	Percent	16	17	17	16
Black or African American	Number	6,533,000	6,509,000	6,493,000	6,427,000
	Percent	66	67	67	67
Hispanic or Latino	Number	6,674,000	6,890,000	7,008,000	7,044,000
	Percent	41	42	42	42
White (Non-Hispanic)	Number	9,329,000	9,466,000	9,358,000	9,289,000
	Percent	24	25	25	25
Two or more races	Number	1,586,000	1,655,000	1,703,000	1,758,000
	Percent	42	42	43	43

Source: Population Reference Bureau, analysis of data from the U.S. Census Bureau, Census 2000 Supplementary Survey, 2001 Supplementary Survey, 2002 through 2013 American Community Survey.

Some adults reach their late 30s or early 40s without finding "that special person" to share their lives with. Maybe they were more focused on work than on dating. Or maybe they dated a lot but just never met the right partner. Whatever the reason, sometimes these adults—usually this happens to women, but it could be a man—decide to become parents on their own. They might take in a foster child, they might adopt a child or even several children, or they might get pregnant on purpose.

There was a time in history when being an unmarried mom or dad was considered to be scandalous. Nowadays, in part because there are single parents everywhere, most people don't find it shocking. It should be said that in some religious communities, the decision to have a child "out of wedlock" is still viewed as inappropriate if not downright sinful. However as the majority of Americans have become more **secular** in their views, the idea that unwed parents are shocking has begun to fade for most people.

Widowed. Sometimes a perfectly happy marriage is brought to an end when one of the parents dies. This is heartbreaking for everyone—and in a unique way

Unmarried versus Single

Some couples live and have children together but, for whatever reason, decide not to marry. Until recently, gay and lesbian parents had no choice but to be "unmarried parents," too, simply because the law did not allow them to wed. The most recent U.S. census found more than 3 million kids being raised by couples who live together without marrying. But although these are *technically* "unmarried" parents, they are not "single" parents in the sense we mean in this book.

Some of the people whom the census calls "unmarried parents" are in lesbian or gay relationships. Until 2015, most of them were not allowed to marry, even if they wanted to.

Of all single-parent households in the United States, almost 5 percent are headed by widowed fathers, and 3.5 percent by widowed mothers.

for the children who have lost their mother or father. The number of people who lose their spouses in any given year is sometimes expressed as a rate per 1,000 people. In 2009 (the most recent year for which data were available), rates of widowhood among people aged 25 to 34 was 1.3 (for men) and 1.6 (for women) per 1,000 people; and among 35 to 44 year olds it was 3.5 and 3.6. But by the time people reach their late 40s—an age when many parents still have children in the house—the numbers go up to 9.0 and 10.2, meaning that about 1 in 100 parents is a widow or widower.

Divorced. A common way that someone becomes a single parent is the breakup of a marriage. There are more than 800,000 divorces or **annulments** every year in the United States—that sounds like a lot, but the totals have actually been decreasing. As with widowhood, the number of divorces is usually expressed as a rate of divorces per 1,000 people. In 2012 there were 3.4 divorces or annulments per 1,000 people; in 2000 there were 4.0.

WHO ARE SINGLE PARENTS?

Nearly one-third of American kids are currently being raised by a single parent: in 2013, 25 percent of U.S. households were run by single moms, while 6 percent were run by single dads. That's more than triple the number of single-parent households that existed in 1960. The numbers among certain ethnic groups are even higher (see table on page 13). For example, single-parent households make up 67 percent of African American families.

A mom and her two kids at the Better Opportunities for Single Parents event at Fort Bliss. There are a large number of single parents serving in the armed forces. The military has programs to try and help these parents fulfill their duties not only as soldiers, but also as moms and dads.

Statistics suggest that married parents tend to be older and better educated than single parents. This is an important fact, because it has an impact on their earning potential. Education and experience are big factors in determining what jobs people get and, consequently, how much they earn. Chapter three will look more closely at the impact this has on single-parent families.

Text-Dependent Questions

1. What are some reasons why someone might become a single parent?
2. What percentage of teen moms are married when their baby arrives?
3. What percentage of kids are being raised by single moms? By single dads?

Research Project

Visit the website of the U.S. Census Bureau (http://www.census.gov/hhes/families/data/children.html) and take a look at their historical data on the living situations of children. Study the various charts posted on the "Living Arrangements of Children" page and make some observations: What do you notice about trends in the past 30 years or so? Have trends varied depending on ethnic group?

It is really tough for kids when their parents can't get along.

Chapter Two

DIVORCE AND SINGLE PARENTS

As discussed in chapter one, single-parent families often result from divorce. You may have heard the cliché that "half of marriages end in divorce." That's not actually true anymore—the divorce rate has been dropping since the 1980s. Even so, divorce is a pretty common event in our world. But it has not always been that way. For centuries, divorces were either impossible or allowed for only the very wealthy and powerful.

Words to Understand

bigamy: marrying someone when you are already married to someone else.

civil: having to do with regular citizens, rather than religious or military powers.

custody: the right to protect or care for something.

heir: someone, often a family member, who inherits someone else's possessions when he or she dies.

lenient: not strict, or interpreting laws loosely.

loophole: a way to get around a rule because of a vagueness in wording.

A SHORT HISTORY OF DIVORCE

History's most famous "divorce" happened in 1533, between England's King Henry VIII and Catherine of Aragon. The king wanted to end his marriage to Catherine because she had not given birth to a male **heir** to the throne. At the time, England was a Catholic country, and the Catholic Church forbids divorce. Rather than submit to those rules, King Henry VIII broke ties with the Catholic Church and established the Church of England. This new religion allowed the King to do what he wanted with his wives. He would have six wives in all; one died from natural causes (Jane Seymour), while two others were beheaded at Henry's orders (Anne Boleyn and Catherine Howard). In addition to Catherine, Henry also dissolved his brief marriage to Anne of Cleves in 1540. However the founding of the Church of England did not lead to a widespread acceptance of divorce for regular people.

The first recorded divorces in the United States took place in the Massachusetts Bay Colony. In 1643 a woman named Anne Clarke was given a divorce from her husband, Denis, who had left her and had children with another woman. This was not the only colonial divorce. In another case, between James Luxford and his wife (her name was not recorded), Luxford was charged with **bigamy**; eventually, his wife was granted a divorce and Luxford was banished back to England. The historian Peter Charles Hoffer argues that the early colonists had very practical ideas about marriage. He says they viewed it as a **civil** contract more than a religious one. This would soon change, however.

In both the Clarke and Luxford cases, the wives were granted the divorces because their husbands had abandoned them. This is significant, because until quite recently, wives were considered to essentially be the property of their husbands. This was a legal principle called *coverture*. Under coverture, wives did not have **custody** of their children, and they did not own anything—not even the clothes they wore. Wives could not keep the money they earned or even sign contracts on their own. They had no real existence in the eyes of the law.

An engraving from 1802 by William Ward shows Catherine of Aragon pleading her case before Henry VIII. He divorced her anyway.

This put women in a very vulnerable position, especially if their husbands left, as happened to Mrs. Clarke and Mrs. Luxford, as well as an uncountable number of other women.

To fix some of the problems with coverture, laws called Married Women's Property Acts were passed both in the United States and Great Britain in the mid 1800s. However, there were many **loopholes** in the laws. It would be a long time before wives were considered legally equal to their husbands. This is why people who supported equal rights for women also argued for making divorce easier. Divorce was viewed as a way for wives to protect themselves from abuse or abandonment.

MODERN DIVORCE

Two events in the early 20th century had a huge impact on divorce in the United States. One was the founding of the Inter-Church Conference on Marriage and Divorce, a Christian organization. Members viewed marriage as a sacred, religious institution, and they declared that people should protect it from secular attack. This view of marriage runs very deep in American life. It can still be seen today in some people's objections not only to divorce, but also to same-sex marriage.

Meanwhile, the first family courts were established around 1910. These are called *courts of limited jurisdiction*, meaning that they only take cases in very specific subject areas. Family courts were devoted to resolving questions of

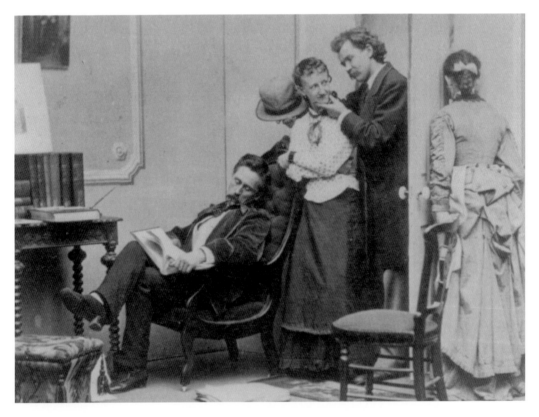

Until the 1970s, couples who wanted to divorce had to show that someone was at fault. Being unfaithful to your spouse was a common "ground for divorce," which is the title of this card from 1899.

After a jump in the number of divorces in the 1970s, rates have been declining in the 21st century.

inheritance, child custody, and divorce. The creation of family courts made divorces slightly easier to obtain, because divorce cases could avoid the larger court system, which took much longer.

Every state developed its own family court structure, as well as its own rules about who could divorce and for what reasons. In the early 1900s, some states, such as New York, limited divorce as much as possible, while other states, such as Nevada, were much more **lenient**. (In this era, South Carolina was the only state that would not grant divorce for any reason.)

But whatever the state, divorce law used to require that one person be considered "at fault." Either the husband or wife had to admit to being unfaithful, to being cruel, or to breaking the marriage contract in some other specific way. Simply being unhappy was not considered a reason for divorce. What happened, of course, was that a lot of couples simply lied, inventing reasons that would satisfy the legal requirements. To end this, California created the first "no-fault" divorce law in 1970. Other states soon followed.

The no-fault divorce sparked huge changes in American society. Now, marriages could be ended simply because spouses agreed to do so. This was either a good thing or a terrible one, depending on your perspective. On the one hand, making divorce easy meant that people had more control over their lives. Research has shown that domestic violence and suicide both declined once no-fault divorce became available. On the other hand, some argue that easy divorce has have made marriage less valuable, leading some people to give up sooner than they would have otherwise. But good or bad, no-fault divorce has been a reality for 40 years. And it has led to the creation of millions of single parents.

CUSTODY AGREEMENTS

When a married couple decides to divorce, they have to make decisions about how to divide everything that they own. This is always a challenging process. But if the couple has children, then the situation can quickly become extremely complicated. Deciding who gets to keep a particular object might be hard, but

Deciding Custody

In custody disputes, judges make decisions based on what outcome would most benefit the child. There are a lot of factors to consider, including:

- the age and maturity of the child
- the degree of the child's attachment to each parent
- the physical and mental health of the parents
- the stability of the parents (this can include financial, social, or emotional factors)
- any history of abuse or violence in the home

The wishes of the children are taken into account as well. Kids who are over age 12 or 14 (depending on the state) have the right to express their wishes to the court.

Case Study: Becky and Rob

Becky and Rob divorced last year after eight years of marriage. They have two young children—Hannah, age 6, and Billy, age 3.

Becky and Rob agreed to share legal custody, but Becky has sole physical custody. Soon, Becky got a job that was about 150 miles away from where Rob lives. The parents agreed on a visitation schedule. Rob and Becky meet halfway between their two homes to drop off and pick up the kids.

"We try to be flexible with each other's schedules," Becky says. "[But] it's not always easy. I hate to have the children from me, so far away." For the children, it's easier. "They love their dad," Becky says, "and they look forward to going to see him."

For now, the visitation schedule is working, and the children seem happy and well adjusted. But Becky worries about what changes the future might bring. "Hannah has already shed tears over missing birthday parties on weekends when she was at Rob's. . . . And as she and Billy get older, I'm afraid they will miss out on team sports and social events."

The truth is, even when a family has worked out a system that works for now, the family may need to adjust it later. But Becky is optimistic: "All kinds of family arrangements can work if people love each other and try to do their best."

—Adapted from *Single-Parent Families* by Rae Simons (Mason Crest, 2010)

deciding who gets to keep a child can be nearly impossible. If the divorcing couple can't agree on custody matters, these questions will be decided in family court.

Legal custody refers to who can make big decisions about the child, such as where the child goes to school, what doctor the child sees and what medical procedures are allowed, and even what religion the child follows. Many divorced

Parents who don't have physical custody of their kids can still arrange for visits.

parents share legal custody of their children—this is called *joint custody*. It means that both parents must be consulted on big decisions. Some families have *split custody*, where one parent has custody of one kid (or more) and the other parent has custody of the others.

Physical custody is often separated from legal custody. Physical custody refers to where the child lives the majority of the time. It is possible for parents to have *joint physical custody* of their children if they live close to each other. But it's not uncommon for one parent to have sole physical custody even if the legal custody is shared. A parent with physical custody is called the *custodial parent*, and one without it is called the *noncustodial parent*.

Noncustodial parents do still have other rights. *Visitation* (sometimes called "parenting time") refers to whatever plans the parents make for the noncustodial parent to spend time with their kids. Usually, custodial parents must seek permission from the other parent to move the child out of state. Noncustodial parents usually also have responsibilities, such as providing financial support ("child support").

Specifics of custody law can vary a lot depending on the state. For example, some states instruct judges to always grant joint custody unless it can be proven that it's definitely not a good idea. Other states give judges more leeway to decide on their own.

Text-Dependent Questions

1. What is no-fault divorce, and why was it a significant development?
2. What's the difference between legal and physical custody?
3. What are some factors judges use in deciding custody?

Research Project

Imagine that you live in the 1970s, and your state is considering whether to allow no-fault divorce. Write an editorial that argues either for or against this law. Find out more about the history of divorce to gather evidence to support your argument.

It's challenging for single parents to balance work and kids.

Chapter Three

SINGLE PARENTS AND ECONOMICS

There are a lot of different opinions about whether the increase in single parents is bad or not. But at least one thing is not disputed: being a single parent is not good for a family's finances. Single parents live in what one writer called "a different **socioeconomic** pool" from married ones. This is especially true for single moms.

In one 2012 study, analysts looked at the difference in earnings between four groups of women: single women without children, married women without children, single women with children, and married women with children. The average difference in income between single and married women without children was $857. But the average difference in income between single moms and married moms was almost $19,000.

Words to Understand

flexible: able to change easily.

socioeconomic: relating to both social factors (such as race and ethnicity) as well as financial factors (such as class).

There are a few reasons why this happens. In a lot of situations, single parents were less well-off to begin with, before kids were even in the picture. In 2013, 1.6 million babies were born to unmarried mothers; of those, 15 percent were born to teenagers and 37 percent were born to women between 20 and 24 years old. It's logical that these young women are, on the whole, less financially secure than women in their 30s. They simply have not had time to complete their educations

Case Study: Donald

Donald doesn't remember his mother; she died when he was a baby. For as long as he can remember, it's just been Donald and his dad. "I couldn't imagine why anyone would need a mother. I'd spend the night with friends, and their mothers would always act so sorry for me—but I thought it was fun."

When Donald was 12, though, his father's store went out of business, and he had to get a job in a factory. "He hated that job," Donald recalls. "He came home tired and grumpy, and all he wanted to do was watch television." For the first time, Donald found himself wishing that his family wasn't just himself and his dad. He thought a lot about his mother during this time. "I had long daydreams about what life would be like if she hadn't died. In my mind, she was always perfect—she would always love me, always make everything okay."

Fortunately, this tough time in Donald's life didn't last forever. "My dad's sister stepped in and helped us out. . . . I'm not saying Aunt Deb was the fantasy mother I'd been dreaming about, but she made us laugh again. We started having fun as a family, going to movies or on a picnic. [I learned that] the hard times are opportunities. Your family can turn a corner and grow in a new direction. And I think my dad would agree."

—Adapted from *Single-Parent Families* by Rae Simons (Mason Crest, 2010)

and start careers. Social scientists worry that once they are responsible for children, they may never achieve the educational or career goals they had before the pregnancy.

PARENTING AND WORK

So, some reasons that single parents are poorer have nothing to do with the kids themselves. But other reasons are directly related to the responsibilities of caring for children.

Single parents are more likely to work more part-time jobs or jobs with **flexible** hours. These "nontraditional" jobs often do not pay as well or have the same level of benefits as most traditional 9-to-5 jobs. People in these jobs are

Being a single mom can make it difficult for women to advance in their careers.

less likely to get raises and promotions, less likely to have health insurance, and less likely to have benefits like paid vacations and pensions. But single parents often choose these types of jobs anyway, because the flexible hours help them deal with child care.

Consider this: the average cost of day care is $972 per month, or $11,666 per year. That's just an average: it can range anywhere from $300 to $1,500 per month, depending on the location and the age of the child.

Day care can make a huge difference in the lives of single parents—but it's not cheap.

TOP 10 LEAST-AFFORDABLE STATES FOR CHILD CARE

State	Average annual cost	Cost of care as a percentage of total income
New York	$11,690	45.2
West Virginia	$6,635	39.6
Wisconsin	$7,893	33.6
Arkansas	$5,909	31.9
Wyoming	$7,800	31.6
Hawaii	$8,904	31.2
Kentucky	$5,389	29.8
Kansas	$6,741	29.3
Indiana	$5,759	26.6
Montana	$5,301	25.6

Note: Refers to center-based care for one school-age child in 2012. Rates are usually higher for infants and lower for school-aged kids. For infant care, the top five least-affordable states were Oregon, Massachusetts, New York, Minnesota, and Illinois; for school-aged kids, the top five were the same but in a different order: New York, Oregon, Massachusetts, Minnesota, and Illinois.
Source: Single Mother Guide (https://singlemotherguide.com/cost-of-child-care/).

Let's imagine a single mom with a four-year-old child. And let's say she has to pay the average amount for child care, which works out to $243.50 per week. She may need a car to get to and from her job—that means gas money, insurance, plus any repairs. As a single mom, she can't risk being unreachable, so a cell phone is probably required—that's another monthly bill. Does she need specific types of clothes for work? That's more money. Whatever job she has must cover all these costs, *plus* rent, food, clothes, and everything else.

But don't forget what else we noted in chapter one: single mothers are frequently less educated than their married counterparts. This may limit the types of jobs that our single mom can get. If our single mom has a minimum wage job ($7.25/hour), she has to work 34 hours *just to cover the child care*. That is an extreme example, but it highlights a dilemma that many parents face. According to the online Single Mother Guide (https://

singlemotherguide.com), child-care costs ate up an average of 40 percent of the income of single mothers in 2014.

If that's not affordable, what is the next option? If our mom is lucky, she has a good relationship with her child's father, and he will pitch in. Maybe she has a sister or best friend who also has kids, and they can help each other. Or perhaps the baby's grandparents are retired and able to look after the child during the day. Statistics show that mothers who live near their own mothers are more likely to have jobs. But if the father won't help, if the grandparents aren't nearby, and if the sister is busy? Then our mom has a huge problem. She may not be able to keep her job at all.

Even middle- and upper-middle-class single parents experience big challenges when it comes to their finances and careers. Let's imagine a single mom who is a lawyer. She has no trouble affording child care, but she has to leave work right at 5:00 p.m. to pick up her kids. Other lawyers at her firm can work late. They can also work on weekends—something else our single mother can't usually do. Guess who gets

Many single parents depend on their own parents to help with child care.

the promotions and raises? It probably isn't the single mom. She has to split her priorities between work and home in a way that married parents don't necessarily have to do.

Text-Dependent Questions

1. What's the average difference in income between single mothers and married mothers?
2. What are some reasons for that disparity?
3. Assuming a weekly cost of $300, how much does a single parent have to earn per hour so that child care takes up less than half her weekly income? Less than a third of her weekly income?

Research Project

There are many programs that offer financial and other types of assistance to single parents. Create a list of programs with descriptions of what they offer and how to apply. You can start by looking up the following programs:

- Child Care Assistance Program (CCAP)
- Temporary Assistance for Needy Families (TANF)
- Supplemental Nutrition Assistance Program (SNAP)
- Head Start/Early Head Start

Marital status doesn't determine whether someone is a good parent.

Chapter Four

ARE SINGLE PARENTS GOOD PARENTS?

You might hear stories in the news about the "alarming" or "troubling" increase in single-parent families. To some extent, those words are *value judgments*: they are based on the speaker's personal opinion about what is the best way to live.

Many researchers have tried to figure out whether it is better for kids to be raised by married parents. Their findings are complicated, to say the least: yes, it's better for kids to have married parents . . . mostly . . . but it also depends on the marriage. (This question will be discussed in greater detail below.) But it's important

Words to Understand

nuance: a subtle difference or shade of meaning.

pawn: here, a person used by others for their own purposes.

psychological: relating to the mind and mental health.

quantify: to count or measure objectively.

stressor: a situation or event that causes upset (stress).

to remember that just because researchers are studying this issue in a general way, that does not mean that there is anything "wrong" with your family. After all, there are great single parents and there are also terrible married parents. It's the job of social scientists to study broad trends, not to judge individuals.

UNDERSTANDING STATISTICS AND RISK

Chapter three looked at how single parents have a harder time financially than married ones. But most parents would say that looking at finances is a very limited way to talk about raising kids. After all, lots of married couples would be wealthier if they didn't have kids, too—but that doesn't mean they believe their kids were a bad idea! What about the impacts of single parenting that are not as easily measured?

Many scholars have explored this question. Studies have compared different types of families and looked at the "outcomes" of children in those families.

The children of single parents do have a somewhat higher risk of having trouble at school. But that does not mean that *every* kid will. It just means the risk is greater.

The Case in Favor

Defenders of single parents have pointed out certain factors that might actually benefit kids:

- Kids in single-parent families may have stronger bonds with their extended families.
- They may also feel a stronger sense of responsibility to the household, because more is expected of them.
- They may be better problem solvers.
- They may be more tolerant of others, more compassionate, and more aware of the rest of the world beyond their own families.
- They may be better able to cope with the losses and disappointments that are an inevitable part of life.

Many single parents are tightly bonded with their kids.

By "outcomes," researchers usually mean education levels, health, **psychological** well-being, and so on. In a 1994 study by Sara McLanahan and Gary Sandefur, kids from single-parent families were found to be more likely to have "behavioral and psychological problems." They were also more likely to drop out of school. Other studies have also suggested that kids of single parents are more likely to have accidents and health problems. Of all the different types of single parents, children whose parents get divorced are most likely to have trouble in school, and also the most likely to have social or psychological problems. Kids with widowed parents are less likely to have these problems than kids with divorced parents.

Some people point to these studies as evidence that having a single parent is not as good having married ones. But there are some **nuances** here that are important to understand. First of all, when we talk about "likely to" do this or that, we are really talking about risk. It doesn't mean that any individual will definitely do that thing. It only means that he or she has a greater *chance* of doing it than some other individual might.

Let's look at a specific statistic as an example. In one study, 10 percent of the kids who lived with their married parents were found to have "serious social, emotional, or psychological problems." Of the kids in the study whose parents had divorced, 25 percent were found to have the same types of problems. So, kids with divorced parents do have a greater risk of these types of problems.

It's easy to take these numbers and splash them in a headline: "Children of Divorce Suffer More Than Twice as Many Serious Emotional Problems." But if you actually look at the numbers—10 percent versus 25 percent—it is still a minority of the total number of kids. One could write the same headline as: "Majority of Children of Divorce Suffer No Serious Emotional Problems." But that's not as exciting a headline, is it?

Another reason to be careful with statistics is that they only give you a general portrait of a large group of people—they don't tell you anything about the lives of specific individuals. The studies "proving" that married parents are better tend to assume what researchers call a "low-conflict marriage." In a low-conflict marriage, the mother and father more or less get along. They know how to solve

Sometimes the media exaggerates problems. Divorce is very hard, but it's possible for kids of divorce to grow up just fine.

problems, cooperate, and generally help each other out. It's not hard to believe that a "low-conflict marriage" is a great environment to raise a child. But does that mean that *any* marriage is preferable to having a single parent? What about a "high-conflict marriage," such as one that involves domestic violence or drug and alcohol problems?

These types of life experiences are extremely difficult, even impossible, for social scientists to **quantify**. It's not so simple to say that one lifestyle is objectively better than another. Growing up with a single parent can be challenging. But defenders of single parents point out that those very challenges can make kids more prepared to cope with the real world (see box on page 39).

WORKING TOGETHER

According to the American Psychiatric Association (APA), there are some unique **stressors** that single parents are probably going to have to address.

Kids and parents should communicate about what's bothering them.

First, it's important that both the parent and the kids understand that their family is not going to function exactly like a nuclear family. No one parent can be both mother and father at every given moment—that's just not a fair thing to expect. The more everyone understands and accepts that life will be different—not better or worse, just different—the less stressful things will be.

Second, there are specific issues that may come up for single parents. If there has been a divorce or breakup, there may be bad feelings between the adults. That can make things tough for everybody. It's vital that the adults act, well, like adults. Kids should not be used as **pawns** or made to deal with whatever grown-up conflicts might be going on.

When parents are fighting, that makes visitation difficult on everybody. Even when parents get along, dealing with everyone's busy schedules can still be very challenging. Patience and flexibility are really important in these situations.

It's hard on kids not to spend as much time with their parents as they want. They will probably miss the parent who isn't around as much. Sometimes the result is that when the kids do see their noncustodial parent, it's a high-pressure situation. When everyone feels like they have to "make the most" of every second, that can end up making the visit a lot less enjoyable.

If your parent has passed away, the feelings of sadness and loss can be overwhelming sometimes. Even if you never met your other parent, you can still miss the idea of having a father or mother. It's also normal to miss the parent you actually have, simply because he or she is always working or is too tired or stressed out to play. Plus, many single parents don't stay single forever. Dating presents a whole new parcel of issues for both parent and kids to deal with.

According to the APA, the most important thing for families to do is talk. Share feelings with one another. Make an effort to imagine how the world looks from the other person's perspective. Single-parent families are still families, and they can face their problems together as a team.

Text-Dependent Questions

1. What are some of the risks that kids in single-parent families face?
2. What are some possible benefits of growing up in a single-parent family?
3. What are some of the unique stressors that single-parent families face?

Research Project

Choose a particular family situation that has been discussed in the course of this book, such as divorce, death, or a parent who's never married. Find out more about what advice experts give to kids in these situations. (See, for example, "Dealing with Divorce" on the KidsHealth website [http://kidshealth.org/teen/your_mind/families/divorce.html].) Write a letter to an imaginary kid who is going through that situation. What advice can you give to help that kid cope?

FURTHER READING

Books and Articles

Livingston, Gretchen. "Less Than Half of U.S. Kids Today Live in a 'Traditional' Family." Pew Research Center Fact Tank, December 22, 2014. http://www.pewresearch.org/fact-tank/2014/12/22/less-than-half-of-u-s-kids-today-live-in-a-traditional-family/.

McEwan, Elaine K. *How to Deal with Parents Who Are Angry, Troubled, Afraid, or Just Plain Crazy.* 2nd ed. Thousand Oaks, CA: Corwin Press, 2005.

Roiphe, Katie. "In Defense of Single Motherhood." *The New York Times.* August 11, 2012. http://www.nytimes.com/2012/08/12/opinion/sunday/in-defense-of-single-motherhood.html.

Simons, Rae. *Single-Parent Families.* Broomhall, PA: Mason Crest, 2010.

Online

Children's Defense Fund. "Bridge to Benefits: CCAP—Child Care Assistance Program." http://nd.bridgetobenefits.org/child_care_assistance_program_ccap2.html.

One Tough Job. http://www.onetoughjob.org/.

Single Mother Guide. www.singlemotherguide.com.

Get Help Now

Childhelp National Child Abuse Hotline

This free hotline is available 24-hours-a-day in 170 different languages.

1-800-4-A-CHILD (1-800-422-4453)   http://www.childhelp.org

SERIES GLOSSARY

agencies: departments of a government with responsibilities for specific programs.

anxiety: a feeling of worry or nervousness.

biological parents: the woman and man who create a child; they may or not raise it.

caregiving: helping someone with their daily activities.

cognitive: having to do with thinking or understanding.

consensus: agreement among a particular group of people.

custody: legal guardianship of a child.

demographers: people who study information about people and communities.

depression: severe sadness or unhappiness that does not go away easily.

discrimination: singling out a group for unfair treatment.

disparity: a noticeable difference between two things.

diverse: having variety; for example, "ethnically diverse" means a group of people of many different ethnicities.

ethnicity: a group that has a shared cultural heritage.

extended family: the kind of family that includes members beyond just parents and children, such as aunts, uncles, cousins, and so on.

foster care: raising a child (usually temporarily) that is not adopted or biologically yours.

heir: someone who receives another person's wealth and social position after the other person dies.

homogenous: a group of things that are the same.

ideology: a set of ideas and ways of seeing the world.

incarceration: being confined in prison or jail.

inclusive: accepting of everyone.

informally: not official or legal.

institution: an established organization, custom, or tradition.

kinship: family relations.

neglect: not caring for something correctly.

patriarchal: a system that is run by men and fathers.

prejudice: beliefs about a person or group based only on simplified and often mistaken ideas.

prevalence: how common a particular trait is in a group of people.

psychological: having to do with the mind.

quantify: to count or measure objectively.

restrictions: limits on what someone can do.

reunification: putting something back together.

secular: nonreligious.

security: being free from danger.

social worker: a person whose job is to help families or children deal with particular problems.

socioeconomic: relating to both social factors (such as race and ethnicity) as well as financial factors (such as class).

sociologists: people who study human society and how it operates.

spectrum: range.

stability: the sense that things will stay the same.

stereotype: a simplified idea about a type of person that is not connected to actual individuals.

stigma: a judgment that something is bad or shameful.

stressor: a situation or event that causes upset (stress).

traumatic: something that's very disturbing and causes long-term damage to a person.

variable: something that can change.

INDEX

Page numbers in *italics* refer to photographs or tables.

bigamy 20

Clarke, Ann 20

custodial vs. noncustodial 26–27

custody 20, 23, 24, 25–27, 42–43

   physical vs. legal 27

day care 32–34

   costs of 32, 33–34

divorce 15–16, 19, 22–27, 42

   history of 20–22

   no–fault 23–24

   numbers of 15–16

family courts 22–23, 24, 27

gay and lesbian parents 14

grandparents 11, 34

Henry VIII 20, *21*

Inter–Church Conference on Marriage
   and Divorce 22

Luxford, James 20

Massachusetts Bay Colony 20

minimum wage 33

nuclear families 11–12, 42

school, trouble in *38*, 39–40

single parents

   advice about 41–43

   behavior problems and 40–41

   ethnicity of 13, 16

   finances and 29, 33–34

   numbers of 12, 13, 15–16

   outcomes 38–41

   possible benefits of 39

teen moms 12, 30–31

widowed parents 14–15, 40, 43

ABOUT THE AUTHOR

H. W. Poole is a writer and editor of books for young people, including the 13-volume set, *Mental Illnesses and Disorders: Awareness and Understanding* (Mason Crest). She created the *Horrors of History* series (Charlesbridge) and the *Ecosystems* series (Facts On File). She has also been responsible for many critically acclaimed reference books, including *Political Handbook of the World* (CQ Press) and the *Encyclopedia of Terrorism* (SAGE). She was coauthor and editor of *The History of the Internet* (ABC-CLIO), which won the 2000 American Library Association RUSA award.

PHOTO CREDITS